BFF4L 2016

D0975310

EVERY THING

IS GOING TO BE

OK

CHRONICLE BOOKS

SAN FRANCISCO

HELLO!

WELCOME TO THIS BOOK. WE HOPE YOU'LL ENJOY IT.

Do you ever feel a little down, a little blue, a little bit in need of someone to come along and clap their hand on your shoulder and say: "Hey, it's your day! You are exactly where you need to be!" Do you ever just need a hug? Well those are the times when this book will serve you well. Tucked inside its pages you'll find boatloads of contemporary art, craft, design, and photography all ready to offer you good cheer. Need inspiration to lead a purposeful life? Try Chris Kenny's *Be a Lamp or a Lifeboat or a Ladder* on page 33. Need a reminder to appreciate the beauty of the world? Flip to Rigo 23's *Sky / Ground* on page 42. Need affirmation that you're a good person? Take a gander at Jessica Gonacha Swift's *You Are Perfect Just The Way You Are* on page 25.

Optimism is underrated. We all get so caught up in the *sturm und drang* of our lives. Worrying and complaining become second nature—something to do on the phone, on the bus, while waiting for our number to be called at the bagel shop. One of the million things that art can do—and do better than almost anything else can (okay, except maybe for a smiling baby, or a hedgehog, or dark chocolate, or a smiling baby hedgehog made of dark chocolate)—is to break the cycle of our days, pull us from the fog of our own minds, force us to look and see and think anew.

The decision to make art that offers us, spelled out in words, a discourse of positivity is a bold one indeed. In letterpress, photoshop, pen and ink, needle and thread, the artists in this book dare to wear their hearts on their sleeves; dare to shake off negativity and cynicism; dare to hope, to dream, and dare you to do the same. Will you take up their banner? Will you wave your happiness freak flag in the street? Will you remind your friends that "Everything Will Be OK"? That "Anything I Can Imagine I Can Do"? That "You Are So Loved"? We hope you will. And we will, too.

this is your life......

YOU ARE EXACTLY WHERE YOU NEED TO BE

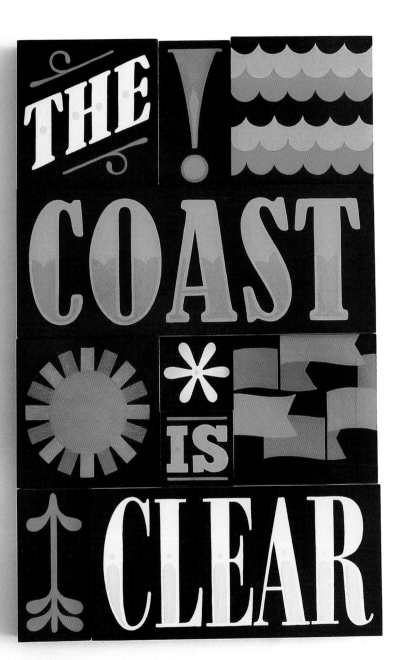

THE! COAST * IS CLEAR

I will fly
to you

©Jen Renninger

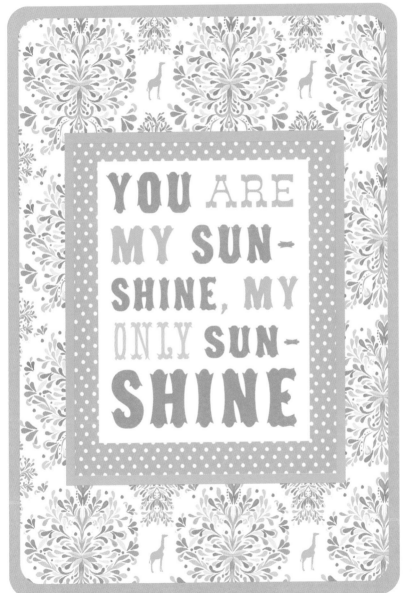

YOU ARE MY SUN-SHINE, MY ONLY SUN-SHINE

Let's FIND SOME BEAUTIFUL PLACE TO GET *Lost.*

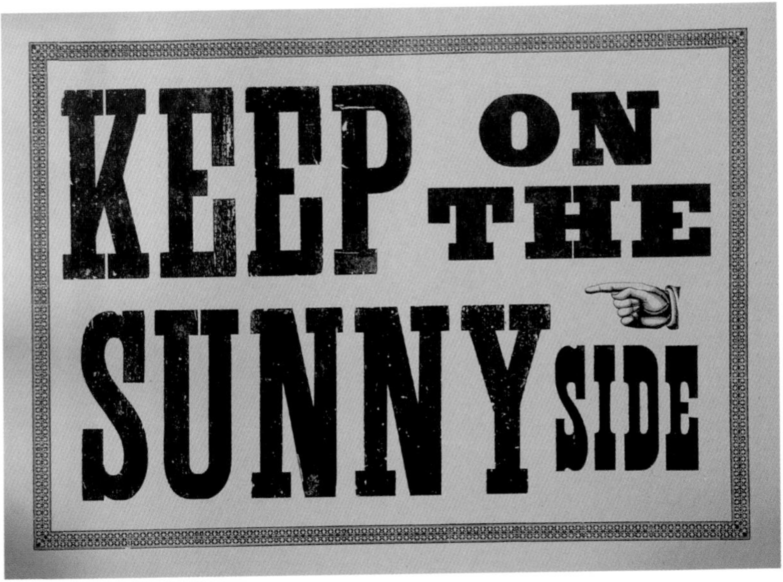
KEEP ON THE
SUNNY SIDE

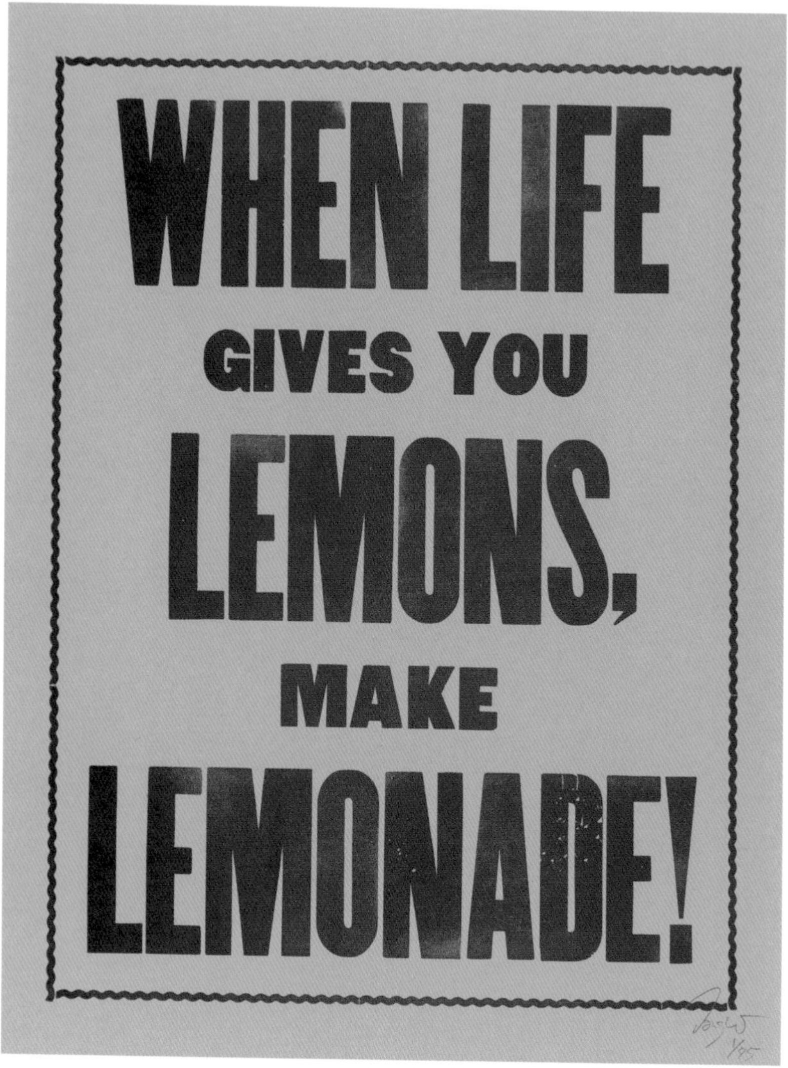
WHEN LIFE
GIVES YOU
LEMONS,
MAKE
LEMONADE!

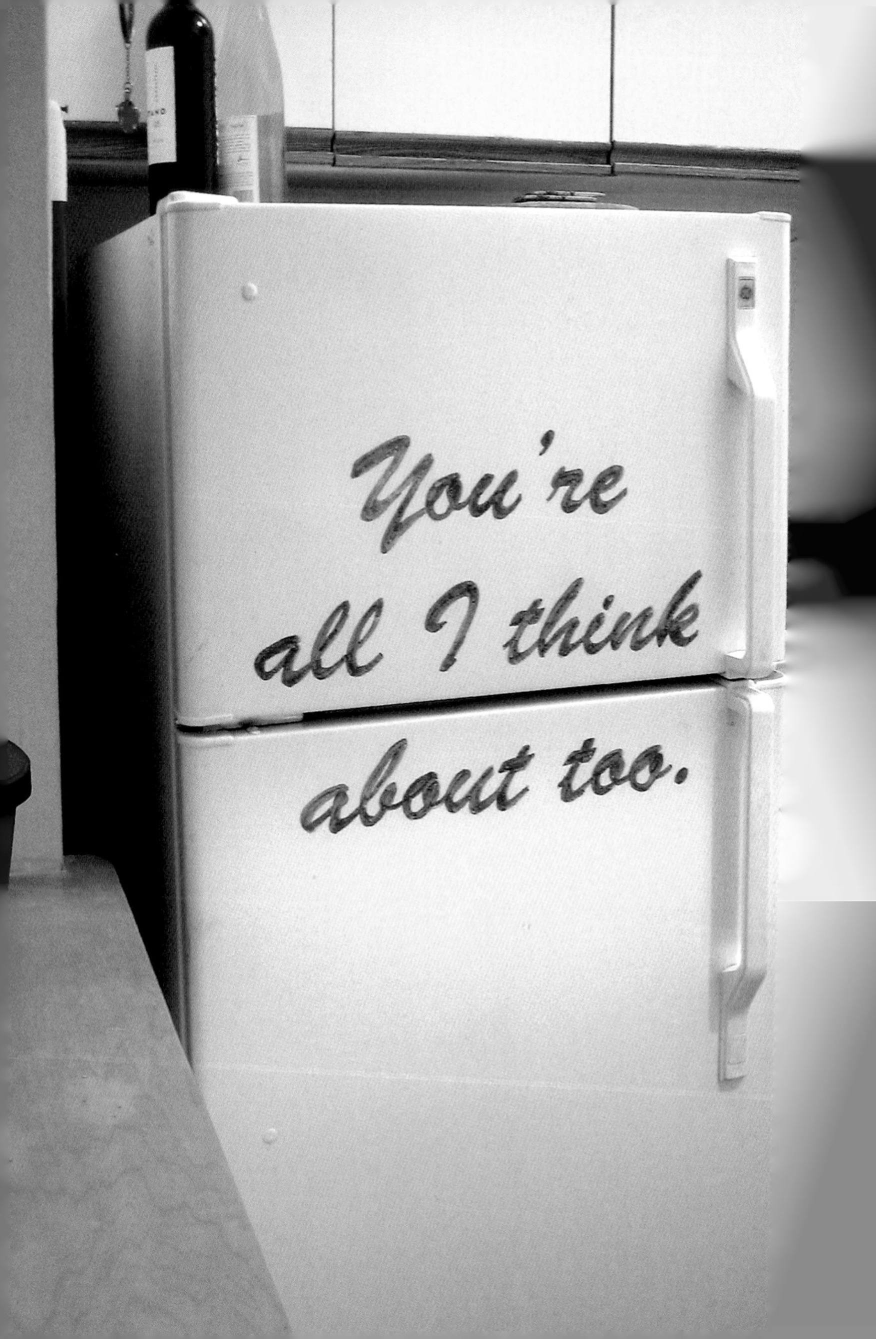
You're
all I think
about too.

BE A LAMP OR A LIFEBOAT OR A LADDER

WORK HARD & BE NICE TO PEOPLE

Anthony Burrill

ALL I WANT TO BE IS
SOMEONE THAT MAKES
NEW THINGS   AND
THINKS ABOUT THEM

ANYTHING I CAN IMAGINE
I CAN DO

IT IS OK FOR ME TO HAVE EVERYTHING I WANT

Anthony Burrill

"One cannot be angry when one looks at a Penguin."

GOOD MORNING SUN SHINE

YOU WILL NEED:

- ☐ CURIOSITY
- ☐ KINDNESS
- ☐ STAMINA
- ☐ WILLINGNESS TO LOOK STUPID.

MAKE IT YOUR HABIT NOT TO BE CRITICAL ABOUT SMALL THINGS.

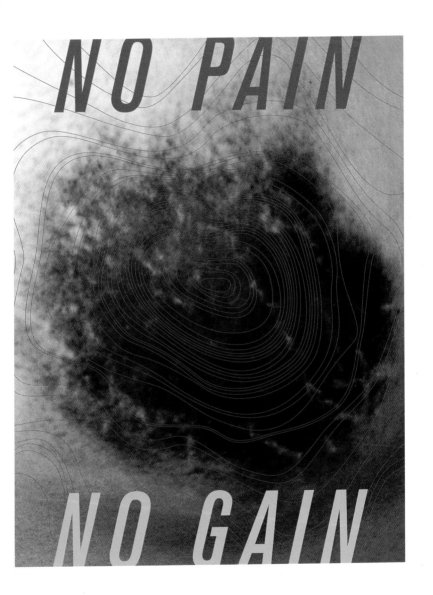

DO WHAT YOU LOVE, LOVE WHAT YOU DO.

MAKE SOMETHING *Good* TODAY

pssst
you are lovely

YOU KNOW MORE THAN YOU THINK YOU DO

Anthony Burrill for the RSA

61

BE PRESENT
EVERY DAY

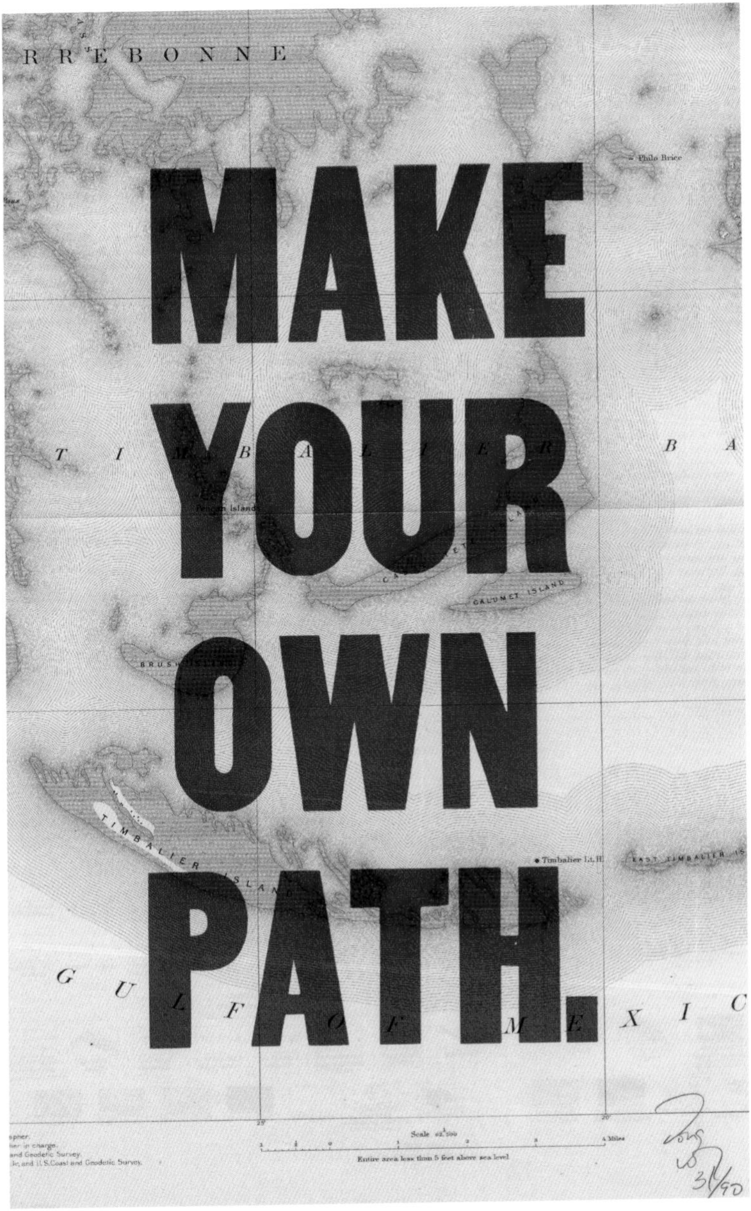
MAKE
YOUR
OWN
PATH.
Philo Brice
CALUMET ISLAND
TIMBALIER ISLAND
Timbalier Lt. H.
Entire area less than 5 feet above sea level
31/90

LOVE IS ALWAYS

LOVE

EFORE YOU.

Stop searching forever, happiness is just next to you.

two birds
never sing
the same
song.

LIVE
WHAT
YOU
L♥VE

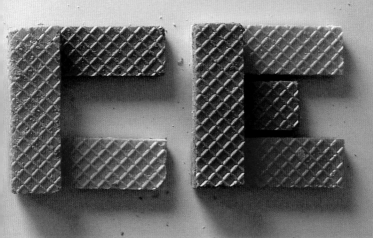

ALL THIS AND MORE

marc johns

IMAGE CREDITS

Introduction and compilation copyright © 2011 by Chronicle Books LLC.
All rights reserved. No part of this book may be reproduced in any form
without written permission from the publisher.

Pages 94–96 constitute a continuation of the copyright page.

All artworks copyright © the individual artists.

Library of Congress Cataloging-in-Publication Data available.

ISBN: 978-0-8118-7877-7

Manufactured in China.

Design by Brooke Johnson

10 9

Chronicle Books LLC
680 Second Street
San Francisco, CA 94107
www.chroniclebooks.com